WARRIORS IN YOUR MIDST

WARRIORS IN YOUR MIDST

Second Edition

"The Lord Your God is in your midst,
A Victorious Warrior."
—Zephaniah 3:17

BRAD REICHES

WARRIORS IN YOUR MIDST
Second Edition
© 2020 **Brad Reiches**

ISBN: 978-1-951648-02-2

New American Standard Bible (NASB), Holy Bible, NASB® Copyright ©1973, 1978, 1984, by Biblica, Inc.® Used by permission. All rights reserved worldwide.

Copyright © 2020
Vision Group, Limited, The

All rights reserved. This book is protected under the copyright laws of the United States of America. This book may not be copied or reprinted for commercial gain or profit. The use of short quotations or occasional page copying for personal or group study is permitted and encouraged. Permission will be granted upon request.

DEDICATION

Max Lewis
Northwest Area Director—Wycliffe Associates

THIS BOOK IS DEDICATED to Max Lewis. Retiring after 34-plus years, Max was the longest-serving Area Director for Wycliffe Associates. He was their 'Iron Man,' with a record of service that may never be broken. It is estimated that Max has driven more than a million miles and raised multiple-millions of dollars all for the sake of Bible translation and furthering the Kingdom of God.

It is remarkable to consider that Max has presented nearly TWO THOUSAND(!) banquets over the years, reaching hundreds of thousands of people along the way. His loyalty, commitment, sacrifice, dedication and consistency over the years have been a model for the entire organization.

Of course, we would be remiss not to mention his better half, his right-hand woman and wife of 54 years, Carolyn.

Together, they will leave a legacy with Wycliffe Associates that may never be duplicated, and will certainly never be forgotten.

ACKNOWLEDGMENTS

(Tony, Brad, Brent, Steven, Noel)

TABLE OF CONTENTS

Foreword—by the Late Don Richardson xi

Preface xii

Introduction xv

A Day's Trek to Peace ... or Death 1

Comment 1 The Significance of Pig's Butt 9

Comment 2 Death Spears and the Red Hat 15

Comment 3 Did You Know We Were Black? 21

Comment 4 Let The Dead Bury The Dead 29

Comment 5 Two Hours, Each Way, Every Day 35

Comment 6 Four Simultaneous Phone Calls 41

Comment 7 The Airport 45

Conclusion 51

Epilogue 57

Author Biography 61

WARRIORS IN YOUR MIDST

FOREWORD

BRAD REICHES is one of the most remarkable friends I have been privileged to know. With his mind and heart saturated with God's Word, one of his most outstanding qualities is his ability to apply biblical truth to virtually any subject or situation. So, although conversations with Brad begin as two-party interactions, they characteristically become three-party interactions as Brad quotes scriptures pertinent to the topic—thereby acknowledging God as a third participant.

Even more amazing, is the degree to which Brad's heart is moved in knowing that billions of people worldwide cannot share in any such conversation since they do not yet have any portion of God's Word in their heart language. Responding to this tragic reality, Brad served under Wycliffe Associates in its commitment to seeing God's Word translated into hundreds of as-yet-Bibleless languages.

In pursuit of this momentous goal, Brad and his colleagues have devoted themselves to reach the unreached by trekking over daunting mountain ranges, fording swift rivers, and braving the possibility that their arrival among tribal groups will not be welcomed. Sheer physical endurance, combined with belief that the outcome will glorify God, propel these faithful messengers to brave the unknown in some of Earth's remotest areas—be it Nepal or New Guinea or a similarly Gospel-deprived area.

May your reading of *Warriors in Your Midst* inspire you to intercede for the success of ongoing pioneering ventures such as the one described in this intriguing narrative!

The Late Don Richardson,
Former National Banquet Speaker, Wycliffe Associates
Author of *Peace Child, Eternity in Their Hearts* and other books

WARRIORS IN YOUR MIDST

PREFACE

THIS BOOK is about conflict and the power to overcome.

There comes a time in everyone's life when we are challenged to walk a little farther, dig a little deeper, climb a little higher. The Bible says that with God all things are possible, despite the sometimes-severe limitations of our own capabilities.

God's Word informs us that:

> We are His workmanship, created in Christ Jesus for good works, which He prepared beforehand that we should walk in them.
> —Ephesians 2:10

and,

> There is an appointed time for everything. And there is a time for every event under heaven ...
> —Ecclesiastes 3:1

I've written this book for all of those who, like myself, have had an unsatisfactory and inaccurate or incomplete perspective on the bigness of God. I've learned that God's ways aren't just higher than our ways ... They are infinitely higher. His thoughts are not just above our thoughts, they are light-years ahead. And His power is not just greater than mine, it is immeasurably stronger.

Are you experiencing conflict right now?
    God's grace is sufficient for you in that conflict!

Do you find yourself in a struggle?
    You are an overwhelming conqueror through Christ who loves you!

Are the cares of the world getting the best of you?
    There is a peace to be had that surpasses all comprehension!

God's promise to you is:

"I will never fail you or forsake you!"
—Deuteronomy 31:6

Do you know Him?

    Have you experienced His awesome power?

        Have you tasted His amazing grace?

If so, your soul will resonate with the testimony of these pages.

If not, I'd like to introduce Him to you.

"For I know the plans I have for you, declares the Lord."
—Jeremiah 29:11

INTRODUCTION

BUCKLE UP!

You aren't just about to read a book; you're about to enter into the adventure of a lifetime! ... A life-threatening, gut-wrenching, real-life saga that will engage all of your senses and touch the very fiber of your being. Its reading will be fast ... very fast!

I invite you to read this book not once, but three times.

The first time through, read for pure entertainment. Embrace the story. Let its danger, surprises, and thrills pump your adrenaline. Enjoy the ride!

The second time through, read to learn. Find in it what you can about what really happened, to whom, and Who made it work out as it did.

And the third time through, read to use. What can you take away? What can you apply in your own life? How are you now equipped to handle similar adventures when they confront you? How does the God depicted in this story want to be a part of your story?

The action happens pretty quick, and I tell it just like it happened. But the events are not the whole story. So, I follow it with some Dedications and some Comments on certain events to explore who the Wycliffe players were and Who else was involved with all of us ... where ... when ... and how.

As I said ... BUCKLE UP!

A DAY'S TREK TO PEACE ... OR DEATH

*The Lord your God is in your midst,
A victorious warrior ...*
—Zephaniah 3:17

ON FRIDAY MORNING, June 22, 2018, I received an urgent email from our Wycliffe Associates President, Bruce Smith, informing me that war had broken out between two of the *Ontenu* clans in Papua New Guinea right in the middle of one of our Bible Translation workshops. Bruce's plea for prayer and support were especially well received because ...

I was there!

Join me now and experience it with me ...

It's 4:30am on Saturday morning, June 23, 2018. I'm in Papua New Guinea with representatives of the *Ontenu* people, a group of 18—men and women, young and old—who have gathered together to translate the New Testament for the first time into their "heart language" (mother tongue), despite being at war now for several days.

I've just finished up my prayer time and am setting up my punching bag "bungee contraption." With its specialized use, it has largely reversed many of my Parkinson's Disease symptoms. Just as I begin exercising with it, I hear that 'still, small voice' from behind me, clear as a bell, saying, "You need to save your strength—this workout is over." At that moment it wouldn't be honest for me to say that I'm not disappointed ... I am! On the other hand, and in retrospect, I can't even begin to express my awe, wonder, and gratitude to God for guiding, directing, protecting, and providing for my every need along the way.

Just two days ago, at about 10am on Thursday, four of the men had received nearly-simultaneous phone calls while translating the book of Mark. Within seconds they begin to weep, one-by-one. Their clans were fighting again—some have been killed, many more were wounded. In the end, 48 houses will be burned to the ground and *multitudes will lose all of the little that they had.*

Pastor Anthony examining the rubble of what's left of his home

The *Ontenu* people (ironically meaning "we are one") are divided into eight different clans scattered throughout the mountainous jungles of New Guinea, and in roughly six hours, I will become the first white man to 'brave the bush' and encounter these warriors on their own turf.

I have been chosen … called? … given the privilege? … to join three tribal leaders who will go into the bush in search of the offending clan to negotiate a peace agreement. I now readily admit that when Pastor Ken, the spiritual leader of the *Ontenu* people and the man to whom I am about to entrust my life, said "We are going into the bush," I had no clue what that would entail. By day's end I will traverse four mountain ranges rising more than 6000 feet (1.83 km)—and when all is said and done, I will have traveled by foot more than 10 miles (15+ km)! As a 56-year-old man with Parkinson's, to think even for a minute that I could accomplish such a thing in my own strength would be ludicrous. I am about to live out one of the most profound experiences of my life, including the loss of 12 lbs. that I'll never forget, and a supernatural empowerment that I will always remember.

Pastors Ken (left) and Anthony (right) patiently wait for me to rest

Tony Tophoney, my colleague and friend, initially expressed the desire to go along. Ultimately, it would be Tony, along with Tabitha Price (the Director of Translation Services and Research), and Joe Gervais, (the Pacific MAST Regional Director and in charge of this project), going with one group of tribal leaders and me in the other, all of us joining with these precious souls in their quest for peace.

And so, our day soon begins with Pastor Ken dividing all of us into the two groups—the larger driving to the main village to advocate for peace, and to have the unprecedented privilege of presenting to them the book of Mark in their own language. Before day's end Tony, our fearless 'man's man' from Pennsylvania, will confront the clan's most respected warrior, 'England,' face-to-face and help convince him and the rest of his clan to stand down.

Our group, Pastors Anthony and Rodney, our leader Pastor Ken, and me, heads into the bush on foot, to track down the clan responsible for the most recent attack. "See that mountain covered by the cloud?" Pastor Ken asks me. "We will find them on the other side of that summit."

In that moment, I remember thinking, *'You've got to be kidding me!'*

When people invariably ask me, "How high was the mountain?" My response is always the same, "High enough to have a cloud covering the top of it!"

Much to my dismay, this is just the first of four summits along the way.

...

Our arrival at the rendezvous point is completely surreal. We are four men with no physical weapons now facing approximately fifty men with knives, machetes, shotguns, 'death spears,' and some old machine guns from World War II. All told, I guesstimate around a hundred people, including the women and children.

Upon seeing that we have no weapons and hearing that we come in peace, they stand down and actually prepare a meal for us. One of the elders comes and sits alongside me with half of a fresh pig butt in his hand … complete with the skin and the tail still attached. Despite approximately twenty dry heaves that I can't control, but mask the best I can, I make it through the meal without offense (even with the very real danger of eating food that my body will reject, the much greater danger would be to shun this offer of hospitality and suffer the potentially fatal consequences of such perceived disrespect).

After the meal, it's time for our peacemaker presentations—and the four of us speak to the entire clan there-gathered. I feel prompted, but compelled to limit my words to about five minutes, leaving the peace negotiations to the other three men. I speak only of the love of Jesus: a love that is unconditional and impartial, a love that is available to the people of New Guinea just as much as it is to the people of New York, a love that makes no distinction between black or white, young or old. (Incredibly, I later found out that God gave the exact same message to those of us speaking to the people in the other village).

At the end of our speeches, it is now up to the ruling elder of the tribe to either accept or reject our peace proposal.

He places a red baseball cap on the ground and I'm told that if he kicks the hat it is a sign that our offer has been rejected. (And, as one of my congregation members quipped, "It's time to run as fast as you can!")

I must admit that my interest level here was at an all-time high!

However, if he picks up the hat and places it on his head, that means he has accepted our offer of peace and a cease-fire is immediate.

As I watch with tremendous anticipation and expectancy, my heart pounding out of my chest, he picks up the hat and places it on his head. The cease-fire is immediate and the beginnings of a peace treaty are now in place.

All of the men immediately gather around me. They present me with three death spears indicative of respect and submission to the instructions for peace that have just been mandated.

I shake hands with every one of the men and many of the women and children.

Peace secured!

It is truly one of the great and profound moments of my life and I am eternally grateful for this privilege that was extended to me.

Within minutes, I become aware of how physically, mentally, and emotionally exhausted I am. I'm spent, ... toast, ... nothing left in the tank. And now ... it's time to begin a three-hour walk/climb/hike ... to be reunited with Joe, Tony, Tabitha, and the rest of the *Ontenu* people back at their village.

"With man it's impossible …"

...

So, that is the story of that day. Well, at least that is what happened.

Let's look a bit more closely at some of its people and parts to see who all the Wycliffe 'outsiders' were and with Whom we all were playing in the action …

STEVEN BRODY
North Central Area Director—Wycliffe Associates

I dedicate my COMMENT 1 to Steven Brody because it's all about the willingness to live by the faith we profess to believe.

I was once asked in a leadership seminar, "when was the last time you did something for the first time?" The question arises out of the belief that good leaders are lifelong learners. They are committed to personal growth and development.

This trip to Papua New Guinea represented the first time in his life that Steven traveled overseas. Overcoming the fears and anxieties that can so easily be associated with such a trip, Steven modeled beautifully what it means to "walk by faith and not by sight," trusting in the Lord with all of his heart, rather than leaning on his own understanding.

COMMENT 1

The Significance of Pig's Butt
The Factor (Faith)

My righteous ones shall live by faith ...
—Hebrews 10:38

UPON SEEING THAT WE HAVE no weapons and hearing that we come in peace, they stand down and actually prepare a meal for us. One of the elders comes and sits alongside me with half of a fresh pig butt in his hand ... complete with the skin and the tail still attached. Despite approximately twenty 'dry heaves' that I can't control, but mask the best I can, I make it through the meal without offense (even with the very real danger of eating food that my body will reject, the much greater danger would be to shun this offer of hospitality and suffer the potentially fatal consequences of such perceived disrespect).

My Testimony

JUMP BACK A FEW YEARS again with me. It's September, 1997, and I'm sitting along the shoreline of Ka'anapali Beach, Maui. It's a little after 5am and the moonlight is just barely strong enough for me to review the first few days of my new journal.

Actually, I have felt the Lord's prompting to begin journaling since 1993, but for whatever reason, this is my first time to ever actually do it. Having said that, I'm completely dismayed at what I've written—I can't believe this is my writing! The words I have penned are not true. I've been journaling for less than a week and what I have documented is not accurate. I'm lying. *'Why am I lying?'* I think to myself. *'I'm the only one who will ever read this ... I'm lying to myself!'*

I claim to be a man of faith, after all, I've been a pastor since 1986. People believe that I'm a man of faith, no one would ever question it. Indeed, I want to be a man of faith, but my actions tell me something different: my behavior says: I'm not.

> *Prove yourselves doers of the word and not merely hearers who delude themselves.* —James 1:22

I'm deluded.

> *They profess to know God but by their deeds they deny Him.* —Titus 1:15

A very bitter pill for me to swallow.

So, on that beach, on that day in September, 1997, at age 36, I make a dramatic change. I stop kidding myself by thinking that I'm the man that I want to be and I begin allowing my actions to tell me who I really am. A very sobering decision, indeed. The Bible informs me that

> *Whoever says (*if I say*), 'I know Him,' but does not do what He commands is a liar, and the truth is not in that person (*me*).* —1 John 2:4

I don't want to be a liar!

Fast-forward 21 years and my actions tell me that I have become a man of faith.

> *Not that I have already attained it or have already become perfect, but I press on ...* —Philippians 3:12

And I'm now somewhere in the heart of the Papua New Guinea jungle, sitting alongside the chief elder of a tribe from a warring *Ontenu* Clan. He is offering me his hospitality by way of a specially prepared meal. Sweet potatoes, some green stuff, and fresh pig butt. He begins by feasting himself on a piece of pork that includes the skin and the tail still intact. After a few bites of this grisly delight, it's my turn.

To be honest, what immediately comes to mind in this moment is the passage in the book of Mark that says,

> *And they went out and preached everywhere, while the Lord worked with them, and confirmed the word by the signs that followed … And if they drink any deadly poison it shall not hurt them.* —Mark 16:17-20

And I'm thinking to myself, *'Man, I'm living a Bible story here …'*

And I'm further thinking,

> *'By faith, I work for Wycliffe Associates to help people around the world get Bibles translated into their own heart language …*
>
> *'And by faith I have traveled halfway around the world for the privilege of being a part of the Ontenu people getting a New Testament translated into their own mother tongue …*
>
> *'And just today, by faith, I will have walked more than ten miles, climbed mountains, traversed fields and valleys and rivers, all with the hope of helping these people to lay down their weapons and put their trust in God.'*

So, as I said, by the merciful hand of Jesus, I have become a man of faith and I am living in such a way as to become the man God created me to be, the man I want to be.

Thus, there is only one thing left for me to do.

So, I politely say,

> "Please pass the pig."

My Prayer for You!

That you stop waiting and start doing! That you stop making excuses and get in the game! That you be strong and courageous and boldly pursue God's perfect plan and purpose for your life. That we always remember that God was with me through my adventure and is with me today—just as He is now and will be with you in in your adventure!

In Jesus name,

SO BE IT!

TONY TOPHONEY
Northeast Area Director—Wycliffe Associates

I dedicate my Comment 2 to Tony because it is all about the willingness to give our lives for the sake of the gospel. Such a willingness is the fruit of a prior decision.

When it became known to us that a proactive, peace-seeking expedition was going to take place in the jungle villages, Tony was the first among us to ask if he could go along. The danger was no deterrent to Tony because he had already settled in his mind that, like the apostle Paul,

> *To live is Christ and to die is gain.* —Philippians 1:21

Tony is a 'no-nonsense kinda' guy' representing a 'no nonsense kinda' gospel.'

> *Choose ye this day whom you will serve.* —Joshua 24:15

COMMENT 2

Death Spears and the Red Hat
The Decision (life or death)

He who wishes to save his life shall lose it,
But he who loses his life for My sake and
The gospels shall save it. —Mark 8:35

IT'S SATURDAY, June 23, 2018 and I'm in the jungles of New Guinea staring at a red baseball cap lying in the dirt. I have no idea what the time actually is, but what I do know is that in moments it will be time for my immediate future to be determined by that little red hat.

For the past hour, the clan leaders and Rodney, Anthony, Ken, and I have been pleading for peace and sharing the love of Jesus with a tribe that believes their pastor was killed by sorcery and witchcraft (in fact, he died of natural causes). Fully intent on vengeance, they have respectfully listened to our words, but now is the moment of truth.

The red hat on the dirt is owned by the chief elder of the clan. He has placed it there on the ground to communicate his decision in response to our invitation. Whatever he decides is what will be for the whole tribe.

If he picks up the hat and places it on his head, it means that he has excepted our plea for peace and the cease-fire is immediate.

However, if he kicks the hat, leaving it on the ground, it means that he has rejected our peace offering and, as one church member quipped, "it's time to run as fast as you can."

It would be a vast understatement to say that all of my senses are as heightened as they've ever been and my heart feels like it's going to pound right out of my chest. His speech is only five or six minutes long, I think, but it seems to me like hours. So, the moment of decision finally arrives and ... he picks up the hat! The cease-fire is instantaneous. Approximately fifty Warriors now gather around me and I shake hands with every one of them. Three of them present me with what they call "death spears." They are given as a sign of respect and submission to the peace that has just been mandated.

My Testimony

This is the first time in my life that I've ever put into practice the willingness to die for my faith; the willingness to give my life for the cause of Bible translation. It wouldn't be honest for me to say that I was fearful at any point in time because I was not. I fully believed that I was in the center of God's will, following Him the best I could as I attempt to do every day of my life. But what I can say is that, as big a thrill as it is to jump out of an airplane or snow ski off a ten-foot cornice onto a slope reserved for 'experts only' (when you aren't an expert), these pale in comparison to the uncontrollable surge of adrenaline experienced while approaching a warring tribe of fifty *Ontenu* warriors watching your every move while wielding knives and machetes, shotguns, machine guns, and death spears.

Even as I write this, nearly 3 weeks removed to the comfort of my home office back in California, I'm aware that my heart rate has increased and I'm sweating as if I had just exercised for an hour. And I become further aware that my mind and heart are filled with gratitude when considering the privilege that I was given to experience what may well be the essence of Christianity,

> He who wishes to save his life shall lose it,
> but he who loses his life for My sake,
> and the Gospels, shall save it. —Mark 8:34-37

My Prayer for You!

That you would start trusting God! That you would stop giving in to the devil's lies, start claiming God's promises, and know that God will never, ever let you down!

In Jesus name,

SO BE IT!

JOE GERVAIS
Pacific MAST Regional Director—Wycliffe Associates

I dedicate my COMMENT 3 to Joe because Bible translation is all about getting the Word of God into the hands of people for the sake of introducing them to Jesus, who then invites them to follow Him.

I've heard it said that God only gives His authority to those who are under His authority. That said, it's clear to me why God has entrusted Joe with such an influential position in His Kingdom.

Joe is a rare man, indeed. How so? When prompted by the Holy Spirit, He is willing to humble himself publicly by bowing down on his knees, whether it be on carpet, dirt or concrete, to humbly worship his Heavenly Father.

Jesus offers, *"Follow Me and I will make you fishers of men."*

Joe does ... and Joe is.

COMMENT 3

Did You Know We Were Black?
The Choice (to follow)

> *Follow Me.*
> —Jesus

I'M GUESSING IT'S ABOUT 3pm and, save for the approximate 90 minutes that we took to negotiate a peace agreement between the warring clans, the rest of the day will have been spent hiking and climbing, roughly seven hours, all told:

> *By day's end I will traverse four mountain ranges rising more than 6000 feet (1.83 km)—and when all is said and done, I will have traveled by foot more than 10 miles (15+ km)! As a 56-year-old man with Parkinson's, to think even for a minute that I could accomplish such a thing in my own strength would be ludicrous. I am about to live out one of the most profound experiences of my life ...*

And I'm *dyin*, man. We've still got about 4 kilometers to go and *I am fried*. I've got to rest. I *need* to rest! For these last couple miles, I'll need to stop every quarter-mile or so and place my hands on my knees and pray that somehow God will renew my strength enough to climb on just a little longer.

"Pastor Brad!" Ken yells out from approximately fifty yards above me. He sees I've stopped and am hunched over gasping for air. "Pastor Brad, I've got a question for you." I know exactly what he's doing. This kind, patient, and compassionate leader is giving me the excuse to rest as if he has stopped us to ask me a question.

"Pastor Brad, have you ever been to New Guinea before this?"

I don't have the energy to answer him verbally, so I just shake my head indicating that this is my first time.

"Since this is your first time, Pastor Brad, I have another question for you."

I respond with a nod that invites him to continue.

"Did you know we were black?"

I take a deep breath and summon the will power to look up at Pastor Ken and inquire, "What did you say?"

Seemingly amused, he repeats the question, "Did you know we were black?"

Too tired to laugh, I manage a half smile and respond, "Yeah man, I knew you were black."

Smiling from ear to ear he joyfully asks, "How did you know?"

I then shook my head in amazement and replied, "National Geographic!"

(Of course, the truth is that Wycliffe Associates has been in New Guinea for several decades … but I was too exhausted to clarify).

Suffice it to say that Ken laughed and I wheezed for the next quarter-mile as his unique blend of love and leadership empowered me to keep on keeping on.

My Testimony

I learned three things about following that day that have clarified and even solidified my own walk with the Lord. There were three keys to 'successful following' that I will make note of here:

#1. *The significance of hearing.* As difficult, and even painful, as it sometimes was, I needed to do everything in my power to stay close enough to Ken that I could hear his voice clearly. He alone knew where we were going and outside of his leadership and guidance, I was completely lost. Hearing his voice was not an option, it was a necessity. It wasn't just a good thing to do—it was prerequisite to my survival and success!

> *My sheep hear my voice and I know them, and they follow me.*
> —John 10:26

> *And you shall hear that still small voice from behind you saying, "This is the way, walk in it."* —Isaiah 30:21

#2. *The significance of trusting.* I literally entrusted my life to Pastor Ken's leadership that day, and I can only describe his guidance as 'brilliant,' both in his knowledge of the terrain and his tutelage of me. In retrospect, it strikes me that complete trust in pastor Ken was my only option, if I wanted to survive, much less accomplish the agreed-upon goal.

> *There is a way which seems right to a man, but its end is the way of death.* —Proverbs 16:25

To think, even for a moment, that I could have survived in the bush without trusting Ken completely, wholeheartedly, and without reservation, would have been delusion of the highest caliber.

> *Trust in the Lord with all your heart and do not lean on your own understanding.* —Proverbs 3:5

> *He who trusts in his own heart is a fool, but he who walks wisely will be delivered.* —Proverbs 28:26

#3. *The Significance of obedience.* It strikes me that as important as it is to hear the leaders voice and trust in what he is saying, by themselves these are not enough. The key is obedience. It is the key to safety. It is the key to success.

While in the bush and on the narrow path, had I not obeyed Ken's voice I would've gotten lost.

While approaching the opposing tribe if I had not done exactly what Pastor Ken told me to do, in the way that he told me to do it, I could've gotten killed.

And while eating the peace meal that had been so graciously prepared for me, if I had not have heard and trusted and carefully followed every instruction that Pastor Ken offered me, well, let's just say that you'd not be reading this book right now because I wouldn't have been around long enough to write it.

My Prayer for You!

That you would become a risk-taker for God and that His spirit of boldness would rise up within you! That you would know that He is with you to guide and direct you every step of the way!

In Jesus name,

SO BE IT!

At the end of our 'adventure' Pastor Ken extended his arms and grabbing my hands declared, "We are now brothers, my village is now your village."

NOEL DAVIS
Northeast/South Central Area Director—Wycliffe Associates

I dedicate my COMMENT 4 to Noel because it's all about the 'narrow path,' and Noel is a man in whom there is no guile. His yes is yes, and his no is no, just as Jesus instructed.

In a day and age where relativism and an 'ends justifies the means' philosophy has overtaken much of the American Evangelical Church, Noel's lighthearted candor and straightforward approach to life are a much-needed breath of fresh air.

Steve Martin, the Director of Events and supervisor over all Area Directors, was unable to personally attend this trip so, of the five Area Directors participating, Steve delegated leadership responsibilities to Noel, knowing that his character and conduct could be utterly trusted.

Enough said.

COMMENT 4

Let the Dead Bury Their Own Dead
The Path (narrow)

Do not turn to the right nor to the left;
Turn your foot from evil.
—Proverbs 4:27

IT'S A LITTLE AFTER 5am, still dark, and a very warm and balmy day awaits us all here in PAPUA NEW GUINEA as I finish up my quiet time and begin to prepare a makeshift workout area. Startled by the touch, I see that it is Pastor Henry's hand that is gently tapping me on the shoulder. "Good morning, Pastor Brad," Henry whispers with a very solemn voice. "Good morning to you, Henry. You're up early today, brother, what's up?" "My father just died," he says, as his eyes well up with tears. "Oh, I'm so sorry Henry," and I reach out to put my hand on his shoulder. "So, I'm guessing your headed home now? How far of a walk is it to get back to your village?" I ask sincerely. Henry responds, "Oh, I'm not going home right now, I just wanted to ask you for prayer. My family back home will take care of the details of the funeral and memorial service. You know, Pastor Brad, Jesus said, 'let the dead bury their own dead.' I will pay my respects upon my return, after the Bible translation is complete. I won't allow the devil to steal from me and the work that God has called me to do."

• • •

As the sun goes down overlooking the magnificent Kassam Valley here in the heart of Papua New Guinea, my new friend and colleague

Stephen points out a landmark, way off in the distance and declares, "It's right there!" Stephen has brought me up to this plateau in order to show me where his village is located. "Wow, you've come a long way to be a part of this Bible translation workshop haven't you Stephen?" And he says to me, "yes" as he starts to smile. After a bit of an awkward silence, I ask him, "What's up with the smile?" As he remains silent with a slight grin, I'm learning that Stephen is a man of few words, so I move on. "So how long will it take you to walk back to the village when the workshop is over?" And Stephen answers, "on average, it takes me about two hours each time." "Each time?" I ask with a clearly confused tone of voice. "Yes, each night it takes me about two hours to get home." "Wait a minute Stephen, are you kidding me? You walk home every night after the workshop?"

"Yes."

"So how do you get here in the morning Stephen?" "I walk," he says matter-of-factly. "You're telling me that you walk two hours each morning to get here, and then walk back home two hours each night?"

"Yes."

My Testimony

These two stories illustrate the caliber of men with whom I had the privilege to know and work in Papua New Guinea. Men of faith. Men of character. Men who walk the narrow road. Jesus said,

> *Enter by the narrow gate; for the gate is wide, and the way is broad that leads to destruction, and many are those who enter by it. For the gate is small, and the way is narrow that leads to life, and few are those who find it.*
>
> —Matthew 7:13-14

In the bush there is just one path, one narrow path. There is only one way and I was utterly dependent upon Pastor Ken's leadership for both safety and direction. Without his leadership and guidance, I would've been completely lost within minutes. To stray from the path would have been dangerous at best and potentially fatal at certain points along the way.

It strikes me that someone who would argue, "There are many paths you can take," or "There are many ways to get there," is ignorant of both the journey and the destination.

My Prayer for You!

That you never give up, give out, or give in! That you keep fighting no matter what! That you trust that God has made you to be an overwhelming conqueror and has equipped you with everything you need to live victoriously!

In Jesus name,

SO BE IT!

BRENT NELSON
Southeast Area Director—Wycliffe Associates

I dedicate my COMMENT 5 to Brent for while the kingdom of God is about endurance, perseverance, and proven character—Brent is their model.

The book of Hebrews invites us to put faith into action—to "Run with endurance the race set before us," (Hebrews 12:1) and Brent does that.

The Apostle Paul tells us that, "You will reap in due season if you do not grow weary and lose heart," (Galatians 6:9) and Brent displays that every day of his life.

I've come to know this friend and colleague as a man of impeccable character with an uncommon care for others. Without question, Brent's career as an Area Director with Wycliffe Associates has been among the most fruitful and successful, by any standard of measure. Far more significant to me however, is his integrity, his love for Jesus, and his love for others.

COMMENT 5

Two Hours Each Way, Every Day
The Requirement (endurance)

Endurance: the willingness and ability to take one more step.

Therefore, since we have so great a cloud of witnesses surrounding us,
let us lay aside every encumbrance,
and the sin that so easily entangles us,
and let us run with endurance the race that is set before us.
—Hebrews 12:1

"I HAVE BEEN CHOSEN ... CALLED? ... GIVEN the privilege? ... to join three tribal leaders who will go into the bush in search of the offending clan to negotiate a peace agreement. I now readily admit that when Pastor Ken, the spiritual leader of the Ontenu people and the man to whom I am about to entrust my life, said "We are going into the bush," I had no clue what that would entail. By day's end I will traverse four mountain ranges rising more than 6000 feet (1.83 km)—and when all is said and done, I will have traveled by foot more than 10 miles (15+ km)! As a 56-year-old man with Parkinson's, to think even for a minute that I could accomplish such a thing in my own strength would be ludicrous. I am about to live out one of the most profound experiences of my life, including the loss of 12 lbs. that I'll never forget, and a supernatural empowerment that I will always remember.

• • •

Within minutes, I become aware of how physically, mentally, and emotionally exhausted I am. I'm spent, ... toast, ... nothing left in the tank.

And now … it's time to begin a three-hour walk/hike/climb … to be reunited with Joe, Tony, Tabitha, and the rest of the Ontenu people back at their village.

"With man it's impossible …"

My Testimony

A man can receive nothing unless it is given him from heaven.
—John 3:27

As this story unfolds during my 56th year, I've seen a thing or two, and here's what I think I know:

Whenever I've had resources, however they came, their ultimate source was from the Lord.

It is the Lord who is giving you the power to create wealth.
—Deuteronomy 8:18

Whenever I've been a man of character, walking in honesty and integrity, both the power to do, and the willingness to be, were given by the Lord.

And whenever I have been successful in representing and serving Jesus, it was He who enabled and empowered it.

Indeed, Parkinson's has taught me that what I'm doing right now, thinking coherently, using my fingers to type, having the ability to see and read what I've written, the inspiration and motivation, discipline and enjoying the desire to write, the energy, the stamina, and yes, the endurance—the endurance to *over*come, and the endurance to *be*come … these are all gifts from the Lord.

I buffet my body that it may obey me ...
—1 Corinthians 9:27

The righteous man falls seven times and rises again ...
—Proverbs 24:16

You will reap in due season if you do not grow weary ...
—Galatians 6:9

My Prayer for You!

That you take the next step, go to the next level. That you enter into God's will for you and become person God created you to be! That you do it now, live in and for Him, and leave procrastination behind forever.

In Jesus name,

SO BE IT!

STEVE MARTIN
Director of Events—Wycliffe Associates

I dedicate my COMMENT 6 to Steve because following Jesus requires intentional, unshakeable, unwavering focus, and this man embodies this critical quality more than anyone else I know.

The Bible implores us, "Do you not know that in a race all run, but only one wins the prize? Run therefore in such a way that you may win!" (1 Corinthians 9:24) Steve 'runs' to win.

Jesus said, "You are the light of the world ..." (Matthew 5:14-16) In a world that includes bulbs, lanterns, flashlights, headlights, brake lights, *etc.*, Steve Martin is a laser. The dictionary defines 'laser' as "a device that produces ... a coherent beam of light by exciting atoms to a higher energy level and causing them to radiate their energy." That's Steve! A leader with a laser-like focus that motivates and inspires those under his care and supervision to ever-increasing higher and brighter levels.

COMMENT 6

Four Simultaneous Phone Calls
The Key (focus)

*"Do you not know that in a race all run,
but only one wins the prize?
Run therefore, in such a way that you may win!"*
—1 Corinthians 9:27

IT'S ABOUT 10AM, Day Four of the workshop when ...

... four of the men receive nearly simultaneous phone calls while translating the book of Mark. Within seconds, they begin to weep, one-by-one. Their clans are fighting again—some have been killed, many more are wounded. In the end, 48 houses will be burned to the ground and multitudes will lose all of the little that they had.

Incredibly, I watch with amazement as each of these four men hang up their phones, take control of their emotions, wipe the tears from their cheeks, and return to the translation work that they have been doing all morning. One of these men is Pastor Carl and he was just informed that his 15-year-old son has been critically injured by a spear through his right leg. The pain on Pastor Carl's face is undeniable, but he and his daughter will remain here, translating the Bible into their heart language until it is complete.

*Therefore, since we have so great a cloud of witnesses
surrounding us, let us lay aside every encumbrance, and the
sin that so easily entangles us, and let us run with endurance
the race that is set before us.
Fixing our eyes on Jesus ...*
—Hebrews 12:1-2a

My Testimony

Focus: "The clear and sharply defined condition … necessary to produce a clear image."

Job said, "though He slay me, yet will I trust Him." (Job 13:15)

That's focus.

Shadrach, Meshach, and Abednego said,

> *Our God is able to deliver us out of this furnace of blazing fire ... But even if He does not, we are not going to bow down to your idols or the golden image that you have set up.*
> —Daniel 3:17, 18

That's focus.

Daniel continued to pray three times daily as he had always done despite the fact that people sought to kill him because of it. (Daniel 6: 10-28)

That's focus.

When Henry (see Chapter 2), and when Pastor Carl and his daughter, determine that they won't be distracted, detoured, or derailed regardless of cost ...

That's focus on full display.

> *Set your minds on the things above and not on the things that are on the earth …. Fixing our eyes on Jesus.*
> —Colossians 3:2 and Hebrews 12:2a

Focus is what kept me alive in the bush. In fact, it's amazing how easy it is to be focused when you're feeling like your life may be in danger.

I was keenly aware that my life was at risk there in the bush. From the time I set foot on that narrow path, until the moment I set foot in the truck on the way back to our cabin, focus is what kept me alive.

Focus on the things of God and focus on who Jesus is, what He said, and what he modeled.

My Prayer for You!

That you stay focused and live in the center of God's will. That you love unconditionally, and be willing to put others' interests ahead of your own. That you never allow distractions to derail you and that you become the living example.

In Jesus name,

SO BE IT!

TABITHA PRICE
Director of Translation Services and Research—Wycliffe Associates

I DEDICATE MY COMMENT 7 to Tabitha because the kingdom of God is all about grace, (not just, or even primarily 'unmerited favor,' but rather the empowering presence of God, to be all that He's called us to be and to do all that He's put on our heart to do).

When I picked Tabitha up from the airport *en route* to Kassam, it was our first face-to-face meeting. We both soon realized that we had a mutual affinity for the Word of God and a common bond in our desire to follow our Lord Jesus and submit to His ways. We further discovered a kindred spirit in our concern for women in ministry and the humble role that is all too often afforded them by men whose attitudes and actions are dictated by a restrictive theology that hinders women from becoming all that God has created them to be.

Tabitha is a champion for women and I am one of her biggest fans.

COMMENT 7

The Airport
The Attitude (humility)

Humble yourselves ...
—1 Peter 5:5

IT'S 4AM ON JULY 2, 2018, and I'm in Sydney, Australia at the beautiful Adelaide hotel. The other four Area Directors and I have stopped off in Australia for a tourist day as we make our way back home to the United States. I'm up early to participate in my home church service in Pleasant Hill, California, via Skype. It's now moments after the service and I'm chatting with my wife Karen over the phone telling her, "I don't think I'm feeling too well." And for the next 22 hours I neither eat nor sleep as my body is wracked with sharp stomach cramps, a significant fever, nausea, and disconcerting weakness and loss of the dexterity and coordination on the entire right side of my body (due to the Parkinson's), and a migraine headache the size of Mount Everest.

Not until 2am the next morning, does my fever break, the cramps in my stomach subside, and I'm able to sleep—grabbing about four precious hours of rest before meeting the guys at the airport to fly home. Although most of the symptoms of my illness have dissipated, I'm still mentally exhausted, physically depleted, and the coordination and dexterity in the right side of my body have greatly diminished. I'm traveling with one large suitcase, a smaller carry-on, my shoulder bag and the three death spears that were bestowed upon me back in the bush.

The paradox is striking! I'm returning home with stories of great exploits! Scaling mountains, negotiating peace treaties, risking my life for the sake of Bible translation, and so on. Yet, what is equally true is that I did not have the physical dexterity to brush my teeth properly that morning. Nor did I have the coordination to button my shirt without the buttoner tool that my wife bought for me several months back and at the airport, I could move no faster than a snail's pace as the other guys graciously waited for me and helped carry my luggage most of the way. Indeed, I struggled mightily just to get from the shuttle that dropped us off at the ticket counter, to the jumbo jet that was about to fly us roughly 15 hours and two thousand miles back to the homeland.

> *No man can lay a foundation except that which has already been laid, Jesus Christ.*
> —1 Corinthians 3:11

And the foundation upon which Jesus builds His kingdom is humility.

> *But He emptied Himself, taking on the form of a servant and being made in the likeness of men.*
> —Philippians 2:7

God looks to the humble.

> *And to this one I will look, to Him who is humble ...*
> —Isaiah 66:2

God gives grace to the humble.

> *God is opposed to the proud but gives grace to the humble.*
> —James 4:6

Humility is the key to effective prayer.

> *If My people, who are called by My name, will humble themselves and pray ...*
> —2 Chronicles 7:14

Humility is the key that unlocks the door to salvation.

> *Jesus said, "If any man wishes to come after Me, let him deny himself, take up his cross daily, and follow Me."*
> —Mark 8:34

And humility is the key to greatness in the kingdom of God.

> *He who would be greatest among you must become servant of all.*
> —Mark 10:44-45

My Testimony

The essence of humility, I believe, is simple agreement with God. Humility says things like, "I can do all things through Christ who strengthens me," and "I am an overwhelming conqueror through Christ who loves me," and "They will come against me, but they will not overcome me for the Lord is with me to deliver me," and "No man will be able to stand against me all the days of my life for just as God was with Moses You will be with me, You will never fail me or forsake me." (see Philippians 4:13, Romans 8:37, Jeremiah 1:19, and Joshua 1:5)

In the bush, I remember thinking things like, *'I'm not equipped for this, I'm not in shape for this, I'll never make it, the mountain is too high, the valley is too steep, this terrain is too dangerous, I'm too tired,'* etc.

The choices I made that day were very difficult, some of them extremely difficult. Having said that, the choices themselves are really quite simple. Pride says: "I can't, I can't, I can't,'" while humility says: God can, God can, God can!"

In the book, *Injured for His Glory: From Pride to Parkinson's*, I recount a childhood and early adult years marked by a great relative strength that was the fruit of God-given talents and abilities. All too often however, those gifts masked God's glory rather than maximizing it.

More times than not, attention was given to the gifts that I had rather than the One who had given them to me.

Parkinson's has changed all that.

Prior to my trip to Papua New Guinea, my hypothesis was that the reason we Americans rarely see the kind of miracles described in the Bible and experienced by many in other Third World countries is because the majority of us in the United States have little need for God and rarely depend on Him for anything. We are our own providers, healers, and sources of wisdom and knowledge.

That was my hypothesis before the trip but now, more than a month removed and back home and reestablished in my comfort and all of my amenities ….

I'm absolutely certain of it.

Upon arrival back at our camp with both the *Ontenu* peace agreement and our safety secured, I sent my wife an email with this picture attached. Her response was, and I quote:

"AMAZING! Praise the Lord!! Which one are you?"

My Prayer for You!

That you continually humble yourself. That you live a life of sacrifice, service, and surrender to the Almighty God—knowing that what God's started in you … He will finish!

In Jesus name,

SO BE IT!

CONCLUSION

*The conclusion, when all has been heard is,
fear God and keep His commandments
because this applies to every person.*
—Ecclesiastes 12:13-14

THAT'S IT! THAT'S THE CONCLUSION, it always has been. It just took me 56 years to believe it. Fifty-six years to get to a place in life before man and before God where my actions tell me that I really believe it. Am I now saying that I have arrived somewhere or have attained something? Absolutely not! Far from it! My increased intimacy with God has only served to reveal how far away I am from Him.

The Bible tells me that God does not withhold any good thing from those who walk uprightly before Him. (see Psalm 84:11) That being said, two things are equally true for me. The first is that, relative to myself, I've never been more "upright" nor lived more righteously than I do today. Yet, at the same time, the second is that, I've never been more aware of my depravity than I am as I write this.

It's true, Saturday, June 23, 2018 was perhaps the single most profound day of my life. And I will ponder the events of that day for the rest of my life. It was a day in which I did what I've always wanted to do, and I was who I've always wanted to be.

...

On that day, I:

- Trusted the Lord with all my heart and did not lean on my own understanding. In all my ways I acknowledged Him and He made my paths straight. (as we are advised in Proverbs 3:5)

On that day, I:

- Walked by the spirit and did not carry out the desires of the flesh. (see Galatians 5:16-17)

On that day, I:

- Loved others the way I've always wanted to love. The love that doesn't take into account a wrong suffered. The love that never fails. "Greater love has no man than this, than one lay down his life for his friends. You are My friends if you do what I command you to do." (as in 1 Corinthians 13 and John 15:13)

On that day, I:

- Submitted everything I am to the Lord. I resisted the devil and he fled from me. I drew near to God and He drew near to me. (see James 4:7)

On that day, I:

- Walked in the good works that God had prepared beforehand for me to walk in. (see Ephesians 2:10)

On that day, I:

- Went out and preached everywhere, while the Lord worked with me, and confirmed my word by signs that followed. (Mark 16:20)

On that day, I:

- Did not fear for God was with me and I did not look anxiously about me for the Lord is my God. He helped me. Surely, He strengthened me. Surely, He upheld me with His righteous right hand. (see Isaiah 41:10)

On that day, I:

- Spoke the truth in love and that truth made other men free. (in both Ephesians 4:15 and John 8:32)

•••

And on that day, God:

- Was with me just as He was with Moses and Joshua, Abraham and Caleb, Esther and Ruth.

   Just as I have been with Moses, I will be with you, I will never fail you or forsake you.
   —Joshua 1:5

On that day, He:

- Showed me that in Christ I am a new creature. In Christ I am an overwhelming conqueror. And in Christ I can do all things because He strengthens me. (as in 1 Corinthians 5:17; Philippians 4:13; and Romans 8:37)

On that day, He:

- Was with me to deliver me.
  They will come against you, but they will not overcome you for the Lord is with you to deliver you.
  —Jeremiah 1:19

On that day, He:

- Opened my eyes to behold wonderful new things from His law. (as He does in Psalm 119:20)

On that day, He:

- Manifested His power and authority and glory through my weakness.

  My grace is sufficient for you, for power is perfected in weakness.
  —2 Corinthians 12:9

And on that day, God:

Caused me to be the man that I've always wanted to become.

Not that I have already obtained it or have already become perfect, but I press on so that I may lay hold of that for which also I was laid hold of by Christ Jesus. Brethren, I do not regard myself as having laid hold of it yet; but one thing I do: forgetting what lies behind and reaching forward to what lies ahead, I press on toward the goal for the prize of the upward call of God in Christ Jesus."

—Philippians 3:12-14

EPILOGUE

THE FIGHTING AMONG THE *ONTENU* tribal people began with the death of a revered Pastor. Friends of this pastor charged members of the other village with poisoning him through witchcraft. The forces of evil stirred the pot and violence erupted. But the grace of God proved greater. The evil that Satan intended, God has used for good. The darkness of Satan's kingdom is being eclipsed by the light of God's Word unifying His children.

A week after the translation workshop was completed, the team of translators were back in the villages with not only the gospel of Mark, but also several other books, including 1 and 2 Peter, and 1 John to share with their community. The *Ontenu* leaders from both villages have agreed to come together and discuss terms of reconciliation. Their plan is to "seek peace and pursue it." They have a testimony to share with the other villages. They are witnesses to the amazing power of God that transcends all earthly powers.

These events have affirmed for me the miracle of oneness that God intends for His children. Going into the village, to a dangerous, volatile environment, was a step of faith and an act of obedience. It was in our hearts, not to exert any influence of our own—based on the world's standards of class, race, or status—but to honor our Father, by sharing in the trials of our brothers and sisters, and standing together as family—His family. We weren't there with anything else to offer.

I have had the privilege of helping to start dozens of translation projects in dark and forgotten places of the world. Those experiences are all precious to me, as God has revealed more of Himself with each door of opportunity that He has opened. Perhaps that, more than anything else, is why I treasured the two-week workshop in the Papua New Guinea Highlands in the summer of 2018. God delights to surprise us, to stretch us, to amazing us. And that is what He did for all of us as we watched Him work among His people of varying cultures, and environments. We were challenged. We were broken. We were poured out. We were filled up. We were undone. We were empowered. We were brought face to face with His glory.

Tabitha Price
Director of Translation Services and Research
Wycliffe Associates

WARRIORS IN YOUR MIDST
2ND EDITION
AUTHOR BIOGRAPHY

Brad received his Bachelor of Arts degree from the University of California at Berkeley, his Masters of Arts degree from Simpson University in Redding, CA and his Doctorate in International Christian Relations from Vision International University in Ramona, CA.

As a Missionary and Bible translator Brad has been privileged to minister in eight countries including Taiwan, South Korea, Japan, and most recently, Nepal and New Guinea. He served with Wycliffe Associates from 2016-2018 as the Southwest Area Director and National Banquet Speaker Trainer. Brad has had the privilege to train more than two-hundred missionaries and speak to thousands around the world presenting a message of encouragement and hope.

He says:

> At age 57, I find myself at a place in life that only God could custom-craft. For as long as I can remember, my joy and passion has been to 'make disciples' for Jesus Christ and equip others to do the same. Jesus instructed His followers to be His 'witnesses' both locally and globally (Acts 1:8), and as one of His servants, I am privileged to participate in such a calling.
>
> Having said all that, there will still never be any greater joy or fulfillment in life for me than hearing the sound of one of my daughter's voices saying, 'dad.'

As an internationally recognized author, Brad has written five books including his most recent, *Warriors in Your Midst*, here in its second edition, which documents his life-threatening journey through the bush of Papua New Guinea in the hope of negotiating a peace treaty between two warring clans.

Formerly a professional baseball player, Brad was diagnosed with Parkinson's in 2014 and is a volunteer advocate and spokesman for NeoLife Whole Food Nutrition.

Brad currently serves the local church as an Associate Pastor at Parkside Church in Auburn, CA, while serving the body of Christ as a missionary, author, and conference speaker.

He lives in Auburn, CA with his wife of 31 years, Karen, and has two daughters, Alison and Jennifer.

www.ingramcontent.com/pod-product-compliance
Lightning Source LLC
Chambersburg PA
CBHW060043230426
43661CB00004B/634